NATIONAL GEOGRAPHIC

W9-BQT-497

THE BEAT GOES ON

PIONEER EDITION

By Nancy Finton

CONTENTS

THE BEAT

Your heart beats 100,000 times a day. Each beat moves blood through your body. This keeps you healthy. But what if your heart is not up to the job?

BY NANCY FINTON

Your heart works hard. It never rests. It beats all day. It beats all night.

Your heart cannot take a break. Its job is too important. It pumps blood in your body.

You can feel your heart working. Put your hand on your chest. Do you feel a thumping? That is your heart pumping blood!

GOES ON

BLOOD ON THE MOVE

It is good that your heart never rests. Your body needs blood. You see, blood carries **oxygen.** That is a gas. It comes into your body when you breathe.

Blood picks up oxygen. *Thump! Thump!* The muscles in your heart squeeze. This moves blood through your body. As blood travels, it takes oxygen to every part of your body.

TRAVELING IN TUBES

Blood moves through your body in tubes. They are called blood vessels.

Some blood vessels carry blood away from the heart. They are called **arteries.** Arteries carry blood with a lot of oxygen. The oxygen goes to all parts of your body.

Some blood vessels carry blood back to the heart. They are called **veins.** The blood in veins has little oxygen. That is because the body has used it up.

BROKEN HEARTS

Most people have healthy hearts. They pump the way they should. Some people are not so lucky.

Brian Whitlow was born with a heart problem. His heart had an odd shape. This kept blood from getting to his **lungs.** Those are body parts that take in oxygen.

Doctors helped Brian. When he was a baby, they moved some blood vessels. This helped blood travel to Brian's lungs. It let his body get oxygen. The doctors saved Brian's life!

Brian felt good for many years. Then things changed.

Take Heart. *Brian Whitlow had a heart transplant. Ten years later, he played goalie on his college lacrosse team.*

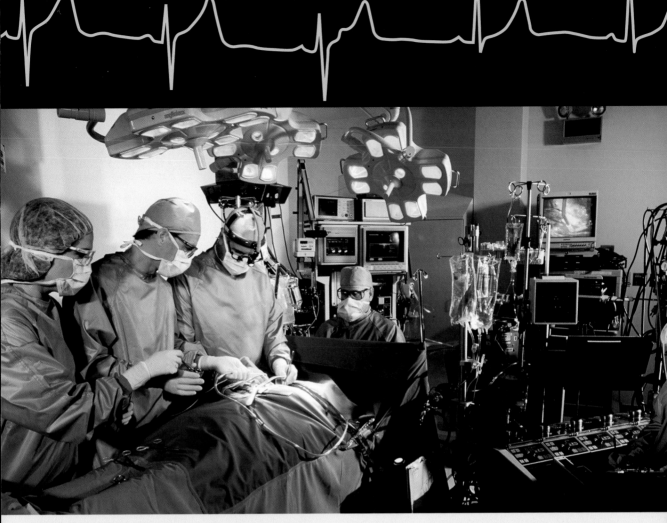

Lifesavers. *Heart doctors save lives. They help people with heart problems live healthy lives.*

A CHANGE OF HEART

By the time Brian was 14, his heart was weak. His body was not getting enough oxygen. He felt tired. He had to take naps all the time.

Brian needed a **transplant.** That means he needed a new heart. But where would it come from?

"New" hearts come from donors. A donor is a person who gives something away. Heart donors give away their hearts if they die.

THE GIFT OF LIFE

Brian waited for 13 months. Then he heard good news. There was a heart for him! Brian rushed to the hospital.

Doctors saved Brian's life again. They took out his weak heart. They put the new one in its place.

Soon Brian felt better. He went back to high school. He played sports such as basketball and lacrosse. The donor heart let Brian live—and have fun again!

HEART ATTACK!

Jessica Melore was born with a healthy heart. But her heart stopped working when she was 16. Why? She had a heart attack. That is when part of your heart gets damaged.

Jessica's heart was hurt badly. It could not pump blood to the body. She needed a new heart right away. She could not wait.

Doctors hooked a machine to Jessica's own heart. It pumped her blood. It kept Jessica alive until doctors could find a new heart.

Jessica got a call four days before the end of school. Doctors had a heart for her. Jessica said, "The heart was a good gift."

Second Chance. *After her heart transplant, Jessica Melore went to Princeton University. She is making the most of her second chance at life.*

TELLING THEIR STORIES

Today, Brian and Jessica are healthy. They are also famous. They have been on talk shows. Magazines have written about them. People want to hear about their lives.

Brian and Jessica hope their stories will help people. They want more people to be heart donors. Many people need new hearts. But there are very few donors. Brian and Jessica hope to change that.

Brian says, "Giving the gift of life is just plain wonderful."

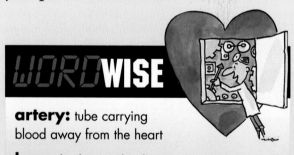

WORDWISE

artery: tube carrying blood away from the heart

lung: body part that brings oxygen into the body

oxygen: gas needed by all parts of the body

transplant: body part that is put in place of one that is damaged

vein: tube carrying blood to the heart

JONATHAN SKOW (JESSICA MELORE); ARTVILLE, GETTY/IMAGES (DOCTOR); ABIOMED, INC. (PUMP)

A HELPING HEART

Many people need heart transplants. Yet there are few donor hearts. Machines can help. One machine helps your own heart pump blood. That is what Jessica Melore used. The machine below replaces your heart instead.

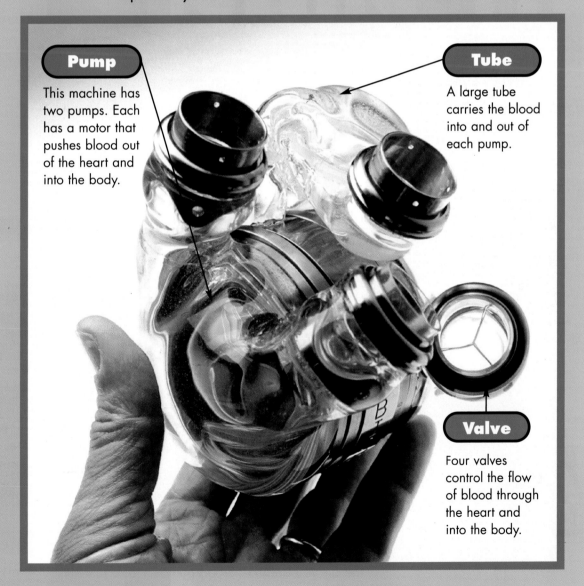

Pump

This machine has two pumps. Each has a motor that pushes blood out of the heart and into the body.

Tube

A large tube carries the blood into and out of each pump.

Valve

Four valves control the flow of blood through the heart and into the body.

Your Circulatory System
GETTING AROUND

Your body needs oxygen to survive. Getting oxygen to all parts of your body is the job of the circulatory system. It includes your heart, blood, and blood vessels.

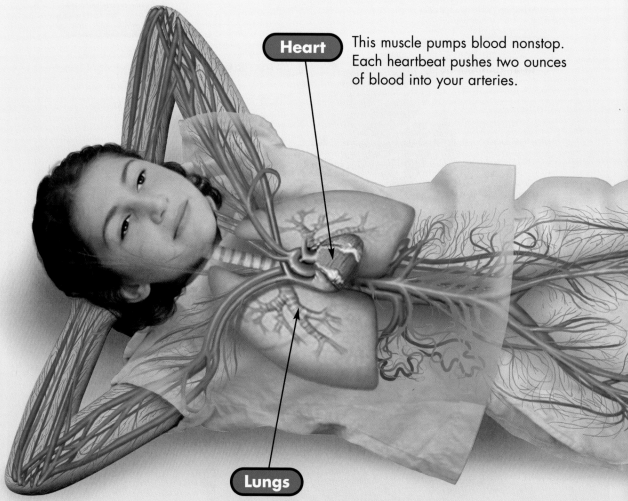

Heart This muscle pumps blood nonstop. Each heartbeat pushes two ounces of blood into your arteries.

Lungs These two organs take oxygen from the air you breathe. Blood pumped to the lungs then picks up the oxygen.

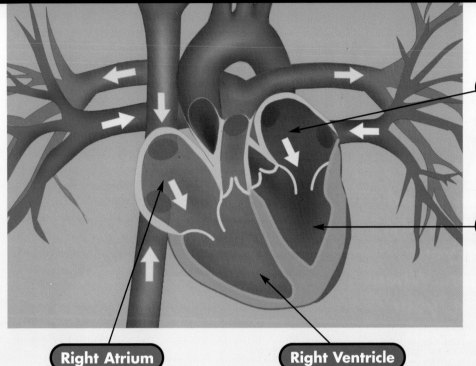

Left Atrium

Gets blood with a lot of oxygen from the lungs

Left Ventricle

Pumps blood with a lot of oxygen to the body

Right Atrium

Gets "used" blood from the body

Right Ventricle

Pumps blood to the lungs to pick up oxygen

Artery

An artery is a kind of blood vessel. It carries blood away from the heart. This blood looks bright red because it has a lot of oxygen.

Vein

A vein is another kind of blood vessel. It carries "used" blood back to the heart. This blood looks dark because it has less oxygen.

PRECISION GRAPHICS (CIRCULATORY SYSTEM); AMANDA BERENY/SELAVY STUDIOS (HEART CHAMBERS).

ALL PUMPED UP

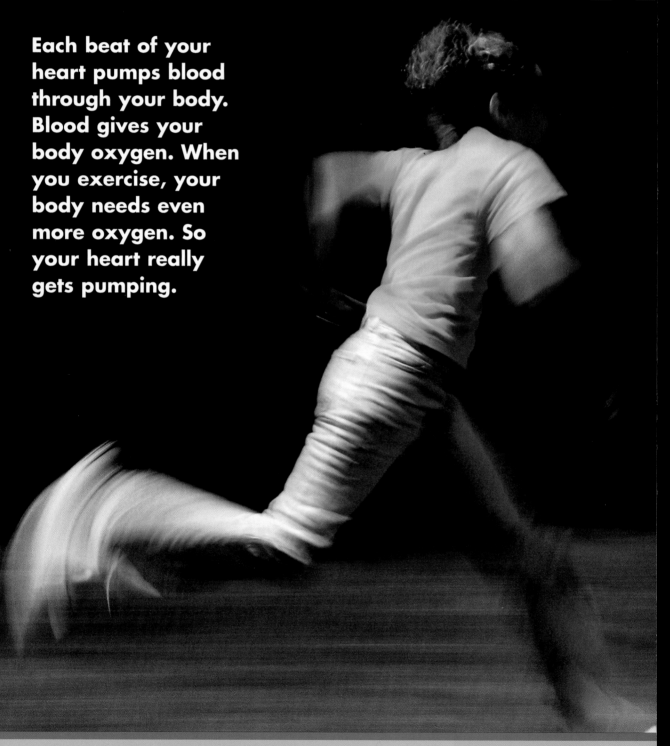

Each beat of your heart pumps blood through your body. Blood gives your body oxygen. When you exercise, your body needs even more oxygen. So your heart really gets pumping.

How does exercise affect your heartbeat?
Find out by doing this easy experiment.
You may want to work with a partner.

Predict

1 Will exercise make your heart beat more or less?

Test

2 Place two fingers on your wrist. Find a spot where you feel a sort of thumping. That's your pulse. Each thump represents a heartbeat.

3 Count how many thumps you feel in 30 seconds. Write the number down.

4 Now run in place as fast as you can for two minutes.

5 As soon as you finish, place two fingers on your wrist and count your pulse again. How many times does it thump in 30 seconds now?

Conclude

6 Did your heart beat more or less after you exercised?

7 Why did your heartbeat change when you exercised?

CORBIS IMAGES

THE HUMAN HEART

It is time to find out what you have learned about the human heart.

1 What does your heart do?

2 What is the difference between arteries and veins?

3 What is a heart transplant? How does it help?

4 How can machines help people with heart problems?

5 How does exercise affect your heartbeat?

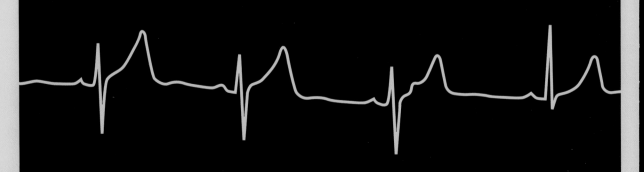